LEGO NINJAGO
Masters of Spinjitzu

ULTIMATE STICKER COLLECTION

HOW TO USE THIS BOOK

Read the captions, then find the sticker that best fits in the space. (Hint: check the sticker labels for clues!)

•

Don't forget that your stickers can be stuck down and peeled off again.

•

There are lots of fantastic extra stickers too!

LONDON, NEW YORK,
MELBOURNE, MUNICH, AND DELHI

Written and edited by Shari Last
Inside pages designed by Anne Sharples
Cover designed by Lisa Lanzarini

First published in the United States in 2012 by

DK Publishing
375 Hudson Street,
New York, New York 10014

10 9 8 7 6 5 4 3 2

002–183710–Feb/12

Page design copyright © 2012 Dorling Kindersley Limited

Published in Great Britain by Dorling Kindersley Limited.

A catalog record for this book is available from the Library of Congress.

ISBN: 978-0-7566-9016-8

Color reproduction by MDP, UK
Printed and bound by L-Rex Printing Co., Ltd, China

Discover more at
www.dk.com
www.LEGO.com

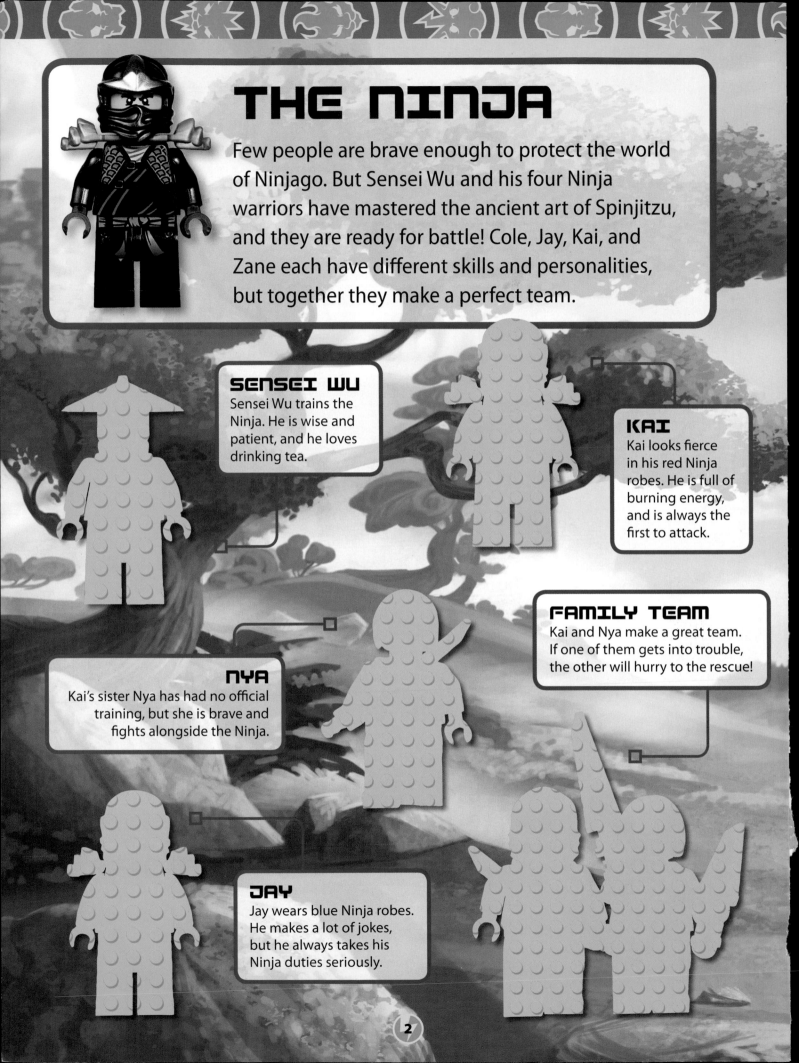

THE NINJA

Few people are brave enough to protect the world of Ninjago. But Sensei Wu and his four Ninja warriors have mastered the ancient art of Spinjitzu, and they are ready for battle! Cole, Jay, Kai, and Zane each have different skills and personalities, but together they make a perfect team.

SENSEI WU
Sensei Wu trains the Ninja. He is wise and patient, and he loves drinking tea.

KAI
Kai looks fierce in his red Ninja robes. He is full of burning energy, and is always the first to attack.

FAMILY TEAM
Kai and Nya make a great team. If one of them gets into trouble, the other will hurry to the rescue!

NYA
Kai's sister Nya has had no official training, but she is brave and fights alongside the Ninja.

JAY
Jay wears blue Ninja robes. He makes a lot of jokes, but he always takes his Ninja duties seriously.

ZANE
Zane is the stealthy white Ninja. He is quiet, serious, and always on the lookout for danger!

SAMURAI X
A mysterious new Ninja with impressive skills has been spotted. But who is under the mask?

COLE
Cole is the black Ninja—and team leader. He is strong, sturdy, and not afraid of anything... except dragons!

SKELETON ARMY

Beware the Skeleton Army! This terrifying battalion of skeleton soldiers lives in the Underworld and they are on the hunt for the four Golden Weapons of Spinjitzu. They work for the evil Lord Garmadon, who wants the sacred weapons for himself, so he can rule Ninjago.

NUCKAL
Nuckal is a fierce skeleton soldier—even if he is not so smart. You can see him from far away, thanks to his huge, spiky head.

SAMUKAI
Samukai is the leader of the Skeleton Army. He has four bony arms, which allow him to wield four weapons at once!

WYPLASH

Wyplash is a fearsome skeleton. He watches from the shadows and waits for the best moment to attack.

BONEZAI

Bonezai is the white skeleton. He has been known to creep up on his enemies without warning. So look out!

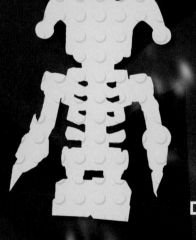

KRAZI

Blue skeleton Krazi is as crazy as his name suggests! He is bursting with dangerous energy and explosive skills.

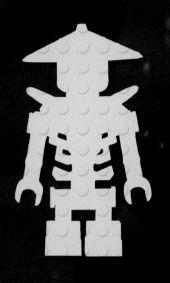

FRAKJAW

Frakjaw is a scary red skeleton. He is full of anger, and he plans to take it all out on the Ninja.

KRUNCHA

Kruncha spends a lot of his time arguing with Nuckal. This grumpy skeleton is stupid—but strong.

LORD GARMADON

This dangerous villain is the king of the Underworld. He sends his evil skeleton troops to do his dirty work.

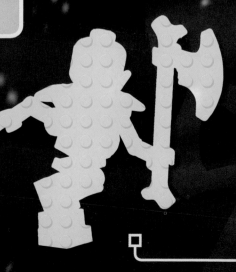

CHOPOV

Chopov, the black skeleton, is so strong and scary, even the other skeleton soldiers keep their distance from him.

FOUR ELEMENTS

Earth, Lightning, Fire, and Ice! The four elements are powerful forces, and they can be harnessed for either good or bad. Both the Ninja and the Skeleton Army can control these elements, but who will triumph when they clash in battle?

NINJA OF ICE
Zane doesn't get hot under pressure. He watches and waits 'til the time is right to attack. He's cool; very cool.

SKELETON OF ICE
Bonezai is colder than cold. One touch from him and your skin turns to ice. Chilling!

NINJA OF EARTH
Cole is solid as a rock—and just as powerful. POW! Watch out for his fist!

SKELETON OF EARTH
Chopov makes even the earth shake with fear! The dreaded Skeleton of Earth leaves destruction in his wake.

NINJA OF LIGHTNING
Jay moves with lightning speed. He can defeat a skeleton, rescue a prisoner, and crack a joke in a flash.

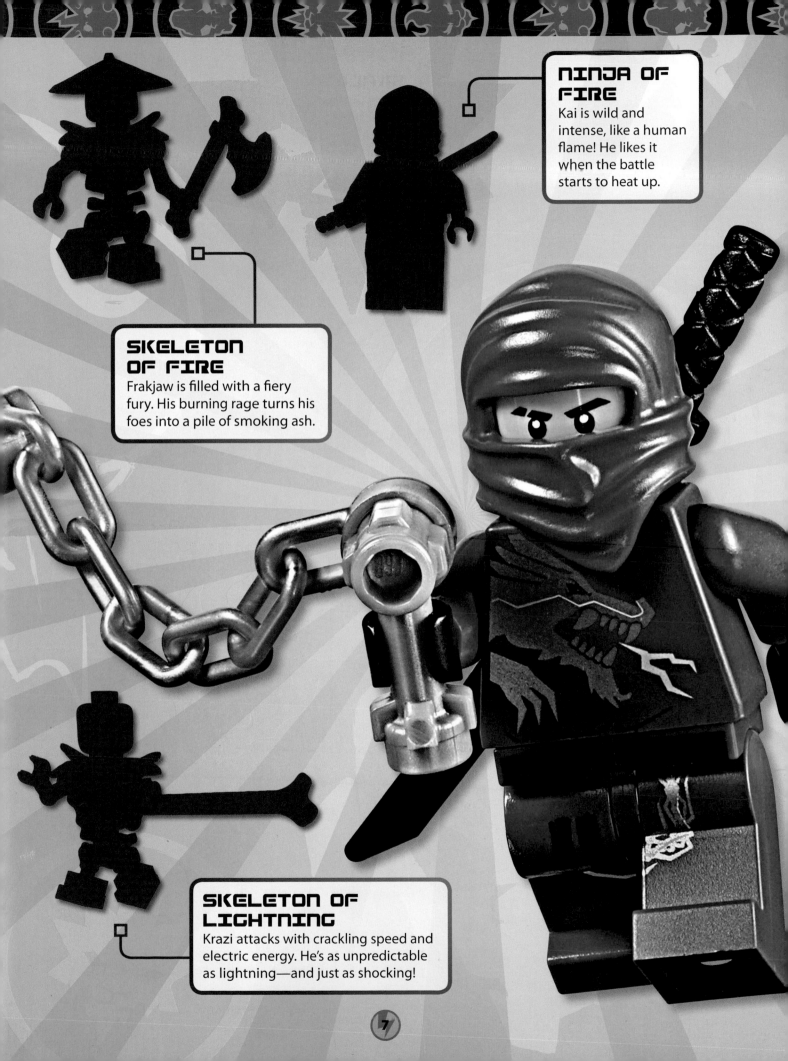

NINJA OF FIRE

Kai is wild and intense, like a human flame! He likes it when the battle starts to heat up.

SKELETON OF FIRE

Frakjaw is filled with a fiery fury. His burning rage turns his foes into a pile of smoking ash.

SKELETON OF LIGHTNING

Krazi attacks with crackling speed and electric energy. He's as unpredictable as lightning—and just as shocking!

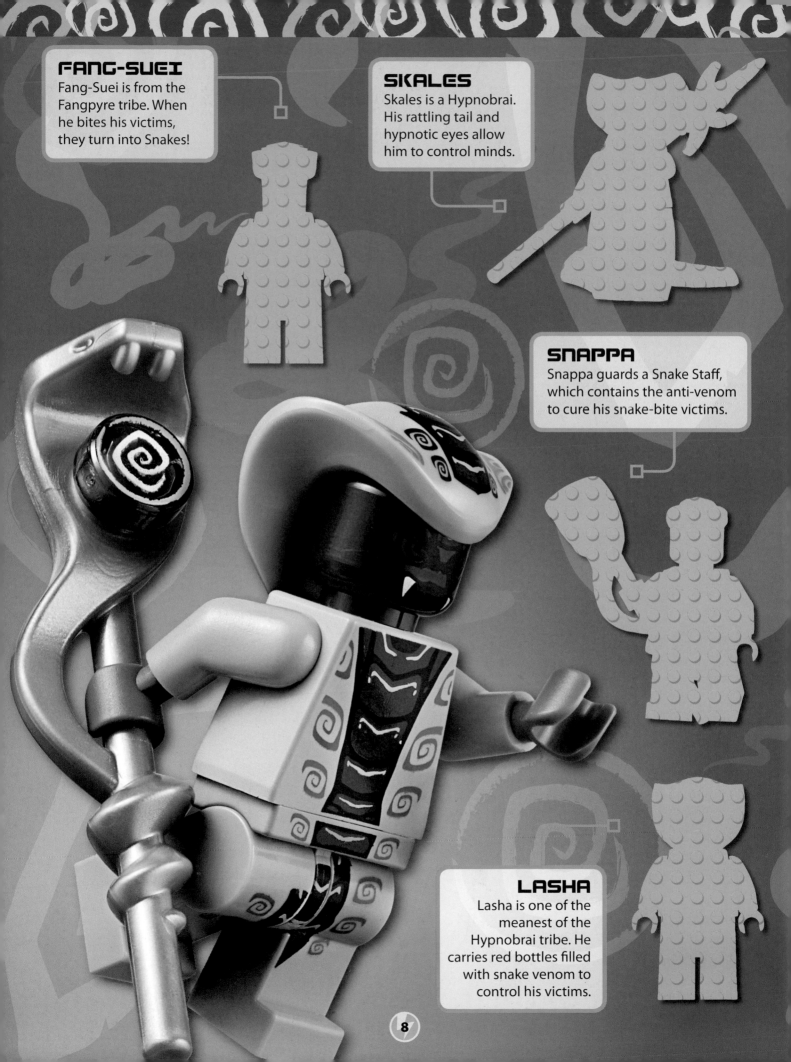

FANG-SUEI

Fang-Suei is from the Fangpyre tribe. When he bites his victims, they turn into Snakes!

SKALES

Skales is a Hypnobrai. His rattling tail and hypnotic eyes allow him to control minds.

SNAPPA

Snappa guards a Snake Staff, which contains the anti-venom to cure his snake-bite victims.

LASHA

Lasha is one of the meanest of the Hypnobrai tribe. He carries red bottles filled with snake venom to control his victims.

THE SNAKES

Watch out for the Snakes! These sly villains slither across Ninjago, searching for people to put under their evil spells. Unleashed by Lord Garmadon's son, Lloyd, the Snakes are a deadly enemy, and it's up to the Ninja to stop them. But the Snakes are not afraid of the Ninja...

FANGDAM
A villain from the Fangpyre tribe, Fangdam and his brother Fangtom are on the hunt for people to bite!

LLOYD GARMADON
Young Lloyd wants to make his father proud. He unleashes the Snakes to prove how evil he is.

SLITHRAA
This sneaky Hypnobrai tricks his victims by pretending he is lost. But when they look into his eyes, he hypnotizes them!

FANGTOM
Fangtom is a competitive Fangpyre. He wants to turn more people into Snakes than Fangdam does. Beware!

RATTLA
It's hard to escape being hypnotized by Rattla. One glance at his red eyes and you're done for!

NINJA SKILLS

Becoming a Ninja isn't just about wearing robes and having fun. There are a lot of lessons to learn and skills to master. A Ninja needs to be strong in battle, wise when making decisions, and kind when dealing with friends.

COORDINATION
Jay can handle two weapons at once—a useful skill for when two enemies attack!

DETERMINATION
The other Ninja admire Zane's determined attitude: he never gives up on a task!

POWER
A Ninja learns to battle with all kinds of weapons—but Kai can also fight with no weapons at all.

AGILITY

A Ninja must have great physical skills. Kai can leap high and twist his body out of harm's way.

LEADERSHIP

Every team needs a strong leader and Cole is proud to take the job! He tells his team what to do during a battle.

STEALTH

Zane is so quiet, he can creep up on people without being detected. It's a very useful skill.

COURAGE

Nya proves her courage when she joins the Ninja in battle against Lord Garmadon.

WISDOM

Sensei Wu always tells the Ninja to use their brains. Strength is one thing, but without wisdom, you just can't win.

TEAMWORK

Ninja must be able to fight on their own, but working together gives them double the power!

SHRINES

There are many beautiful shrines throughout the world of Ninjago. Most ancient shrines are calm and peaceful—a perfect place for a Ninja to relax and meditate. Some shrines are built especially to display sacred weapons or ancient artifacts, while others are hidden away to conceal glittering treasure.

MEDITATE
Sensei Wu likes to meditate at a calm shrine for some peace and quiet!

PRACTICE
Cole visits a peaceful shrine to practice. It is a good way to improve his focus.

SECRET SHRINE
This small shrine is hidden deep in the forest. It is camouflaged with trees so it remains hidden from enemies.

不屈

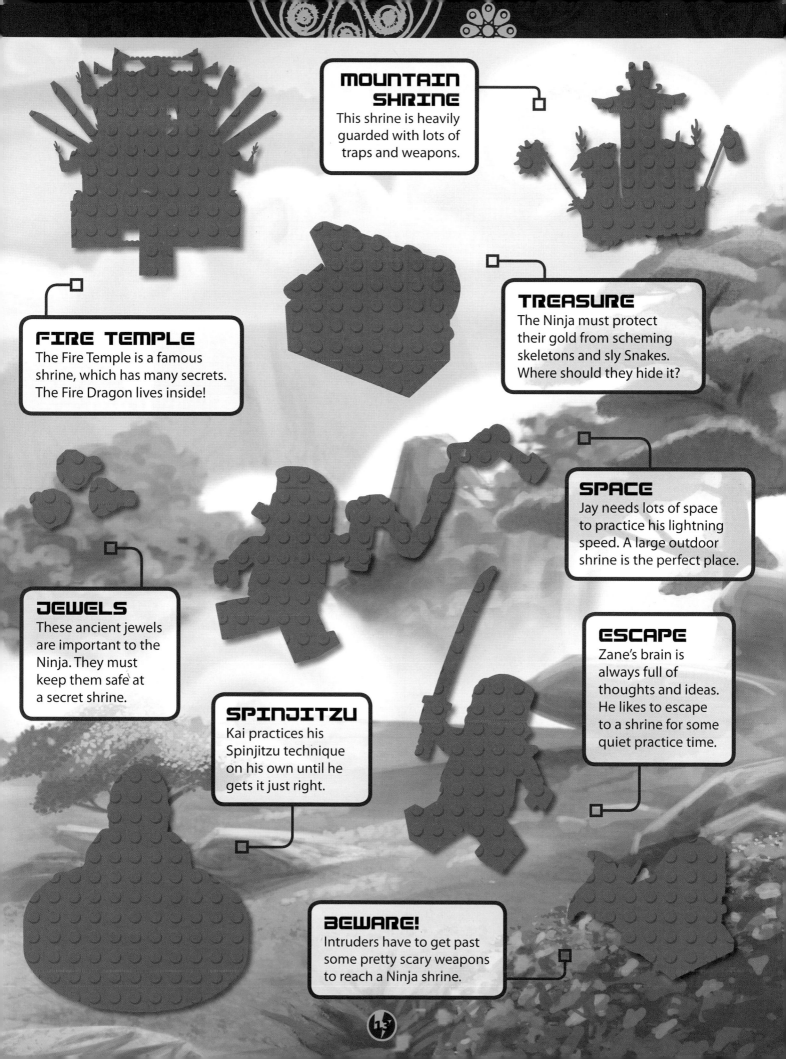

MOUNTAIN SHRINE
This shrine is heavily guarded with lots of traps and weapons.

FIRE TEMPLE
The Fire Temple is a famous shrine, which has many secrets. The Fire Dragon lives inside!

TREASURE
The Ninja must protect their gold from scheming skeletons and sly Snakes. Where should they hide it?

SPACE
Jay needs lots of space to practice his lightning speed. A large outdoor shrine is the perfect place.

JEWELS
These ancient jewels are important to the Ninja. They must keep them safe at a secret shrine.

ESCAPE
Zane's brain is always full of thoughts and ideas. He likes to escape to a shrine for some quiet practice time.

SPINJITZU
Kai practices his Spinjitzu technique on his own until he gets it just right.

BEWARE!
Intruders have to get past some pretty scary weapons to reach a Ninja shrine.

13

NINJA TRAINING

Ninja have to be the best of the best! Sensei Wu makes his students train every day until they succeed at their task. The Spinjitzu Dojo is the perfect training ground: it has lots of weapons, plenty of space, and its walls are covered with challenging obstacle courses.

BLADESTAFF
A bladestaff is good for attacking many enemies at once, but it is dangerous! The Ninja learn to use their weapons carefully.

TEAM LEADER
Cole watches the others train. Knowing his team makes him a good leader.

NEW WEAPONS
Zane trains with a pair of sai daggers. Sensei Wu instructs him how best to use them.

BULLSEYE!
The Ninja learn how to hit a target with a well-aimed throw. Practice makes perfect!

TWIN BLADES
At first, Kai finds it tricky to use two blades at once, but Sensei Wu helps him!

SWORD SKILL
Jay practices with a silver katana blade. It's tiring, but Jay never gives up.

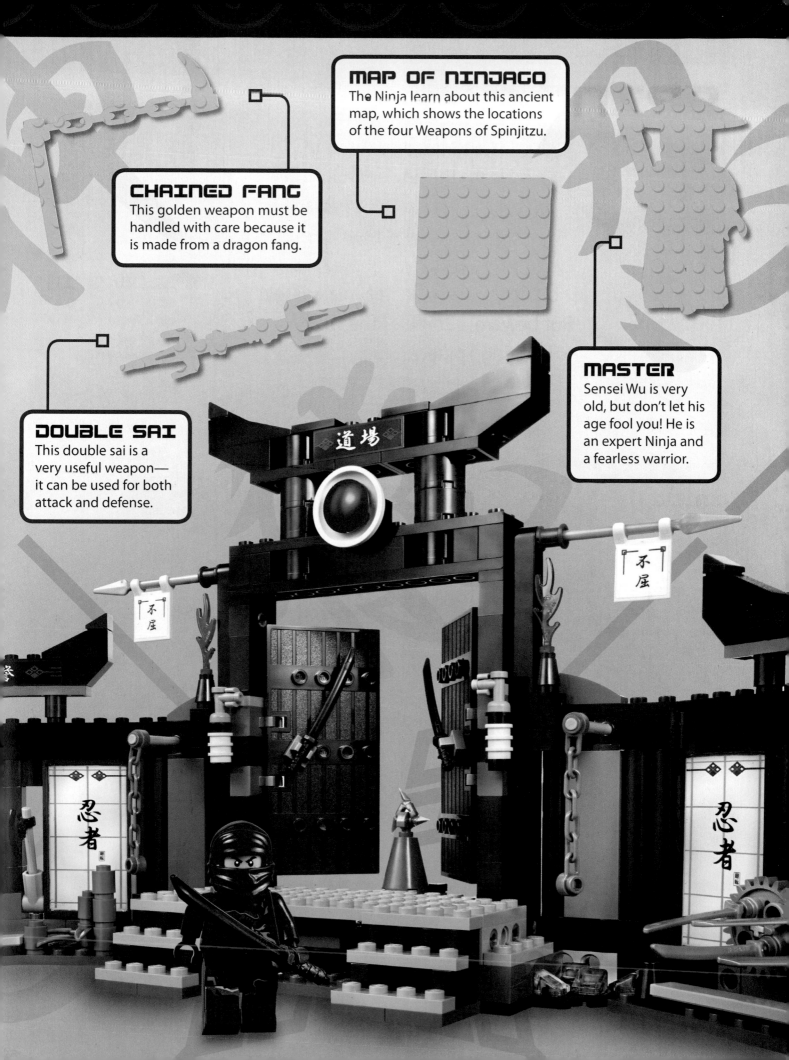

MAP OF NINJAGO
The Ninja learn about this ancient map, which shows the locations of the four Weapons of Spinjitzu.

CHAINED FANG
This golden weapon must be handled with care because it is made from a dragon fang.

MASTER
Sensei Wu is very old, but don't let his age fool you! He is an expert Ninja and a fearless warrior.

DOUBLE SAI
This double sai is a very useful weapon—it can be used for both attack and defense.

SPINJITZU

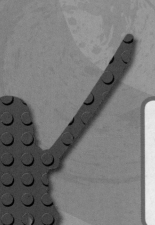

The Ninja are excited to learn the ancient martial art of Spinjitzu. Once perfected, Spinjitzu gives them the power to spin fast enough to become a tornado of Ninja energy! But beware—some of the villains are learning Spinjitzu, too...

SLOW SPIN
Rattla can only do a basic type of Spinjitzu. His tornado is weak against the Ninja!

COLE'S SPIN
Cole's mighty earth tornado spins soil and dirt into a frenzy, reducing everything to dust.

TORNADO OF EVIL
Lord Garmadon's black tornado of destruction is a terrifying sight.

FIRE SPIN
Kai's fire tornado burns with sizzling power, leaving a smoking pile of cinders in its wake.

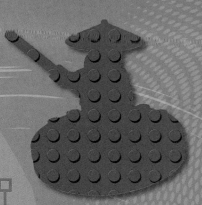

SNAPPA'S SPIN
Snappa thinks he is the best at everything, but he's wrong! He is slow to master Spinjitzu.

SPINJITZU MASTER
Sensei Wu can spin into a superfast tornado—and still keep his hat on!

TORNADO X
Samurai X might be mysterious, but there is no doubt that this Ninja has learnt the art of Spinjitzu!

LIGHTNING SPIN
Jay turns into a lightning tornado in a flash. Crackling with light and energy, he spins superfast!

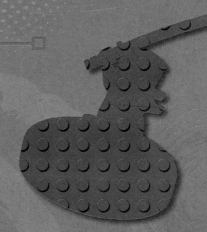

SPINNING ICE
Zane transforms into a tornado of snow and ice. It freezes his enemies in their tracks.

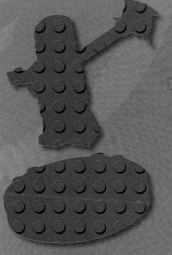

WEAPONS

Scythe, Nunchuks, Shurikens, and Sword! These are the four mystical Weapons of Spinjitzu, which were used to create Ninjago. The Ninja must protect these sacred weapons—but their enemies also have many weapons at their disposal.

SNAKE STAFF
This golden Staff contains the anti-venom for those under a Snake spell.

DRAGON BLADE
Only a dragon master can truly harness the power of these mighty twin blades.

SNAKE POLE
Lloyd Garmadon leads the Snakes with his Snake Pole. The green spikes fire poisonous snake venom.

WEAPONS MASTER
Jay uses his speed and coordination to wield two weapons at once.

GUARDIAN
Rattla will do anything to keep his precious Snake Staff away from the Ninja!

SHURIKENS OF ICE
These throwing stars are a Weapon of Spinjitzu. They cut through the air with icy precision.

SWORD OF FIRE
This golden sword is a Weapon of Spinjitzu. It gives its owner the power of fire.

DRAGON SWORD
When Kai took control of his Fire Dragon, he gained control of this beautiful sword.

CHAINSAW
Cole's dangerous golden chainsaw cuts through almost anything!

SCYTHE OF QUAKES
This scythe is a Weapon of Spinjitzu. It can destroy trees and move mountains.

NUNCHUKS OF LIGHTNING
This sacred Weapon of Spinjitzu is powered by a bolt of lightning.

THUNDERBOLT
Look out! Lord Garmadon's fearsome weapon shoots bolts of energy at his enemies.

GOLDEN SNAKE
The snake-shaped weapons of the evil Snakes can turn into real, live snakes!

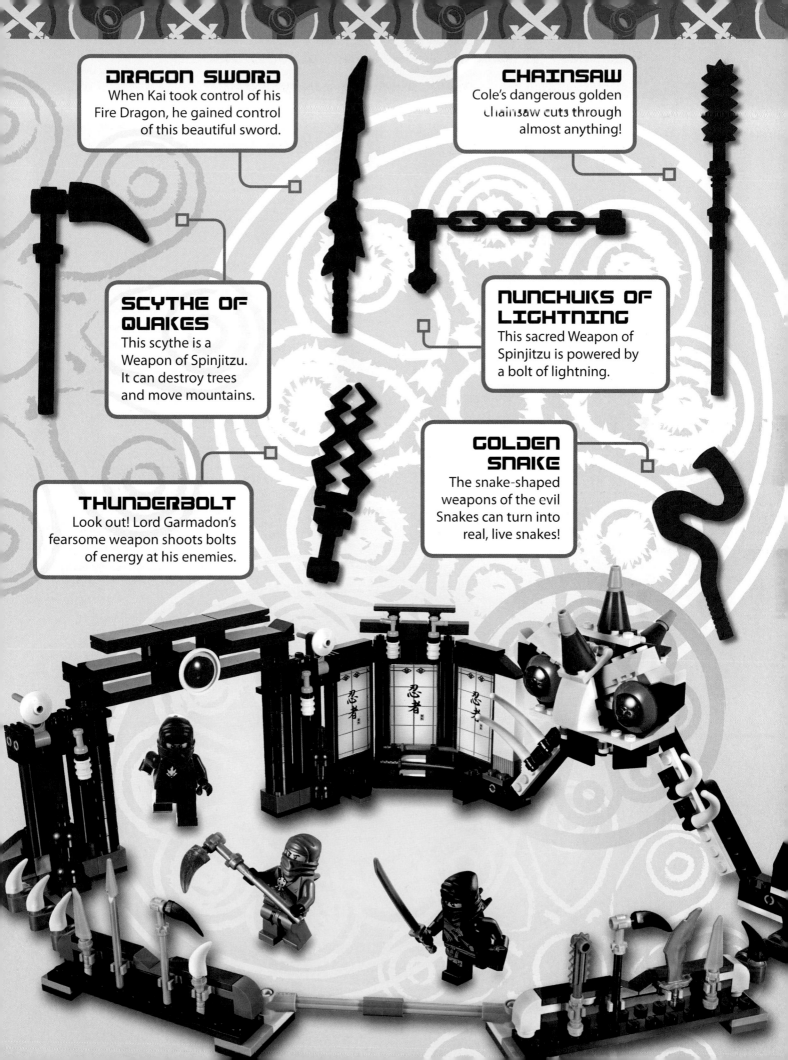

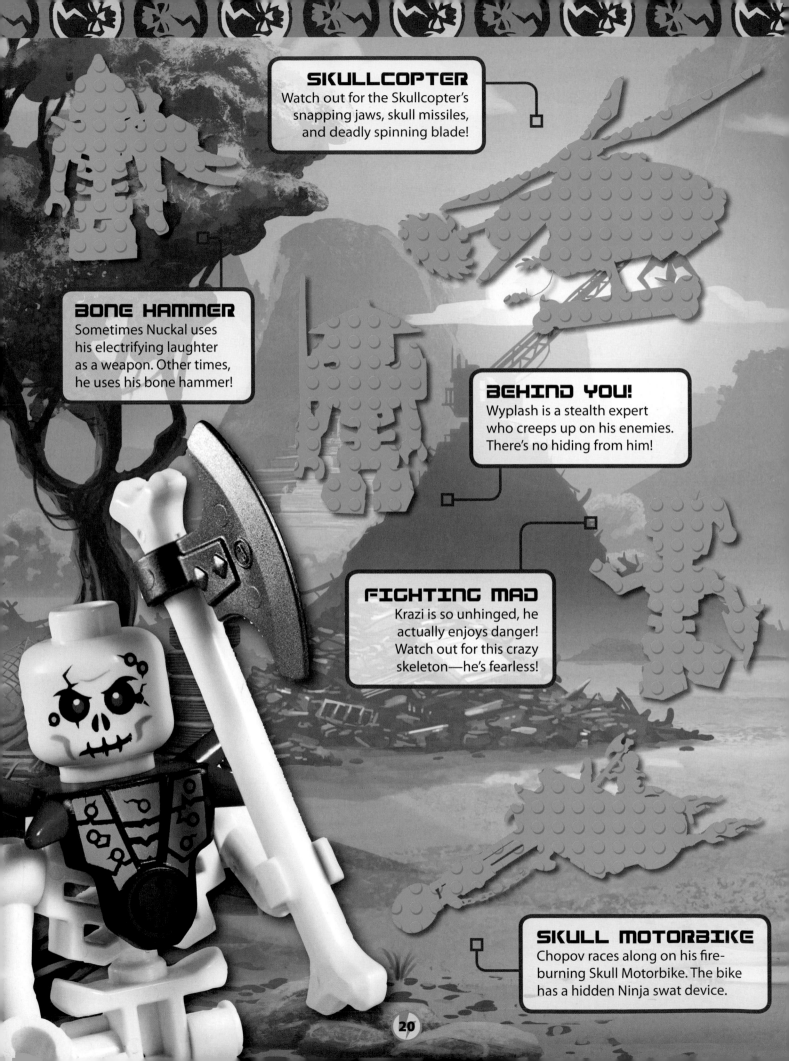

SKULLCOPTER
Watch out for the Skullcopter's snapping jaws, skull missiles, and deadly spinning blade!

BONE HAMMER
Sometimes Nuckal uses his electrifying laughter as a weapon. Other times, he uses his bone hammer!

BEHIND YOU!
Wyplash is a stealth expert who creeps up on his enemies. There's no hiding from him!

FIGHTING MAD
Krazi is so unhinged, he actually enjoys danger! Watch out for this crazy skeleton—he's fearless!

SKULL MOTORBIKE
Chopov races along on his fire-burning Skull Motorbike. The bike has a hidden Ninja swat device.

SKELETON MIGHT

As they search for the Golden Weapons of Spinjitzu, the skeleton soldiers terrorize the inhabitants of Ninjago. They wield fearsome weapons and speed across Ninjago in huge skull-powered super vehicles. Take cover!

TURBO SHREDDER
Frakjaw makes a quick getaway in his Turbo Shredder. Will the flame exhausts help him escape from the Ninja?

NUCKAL'S ATV
The skeleton's All Terrain Vehicle shoots skull missiles at approaching Ninja. Its huge wheels can crush almost anything.

SKULL TRUCK
Keep clear of Wyplash's Skull Truck! It has spikes on its wheels and a pair of crunching jaws at the front.

ROASTING
Frakjaw loves fire. He likes burning his enemies... almost as much as he loves roasted marshmallows!

DARING RESCUE

Danger lurks in Lord Garmadon's Dark Fortress. It is inhabited by Underworld creatures, skeleton soldiers, and Garmadon himself. The Ninja are scared to enter this dreaded place, but they must—because the skeletons have captured Nya! Who will come out alive?

NO FEAR

Kai shows no fear! He charges into the Fortress, searching for Nya. He attacks every skeleton in sight!

CAPTURED!

Nya is helping the Ninja fight off a skeleton attack when she gets captured. She is taken to the Dark Fortress.

BONE CLAWS

Traps and weapons fill the rooms of the Fortress. Sensei Wu is caught within some sharp, bony claws.

PRISONER

Nya is scared! But she is relieved when Kai arrives to rescue her.

GREEDY SKELETON

Samukai is in possession of three of the Weapons of Spinjitzu. What will happen when he finds the fourth?

BONE SPIDER

Enormous bone spiders creep through the shadows of the Dark Fortress. Once they catch you, they never let go!

DEFEATED

Wyplash is no pushover, but he can't defend himself against Kai's fury. This skeleton isn't going anywhere.

CRUSHED

Nuckal tries to use his lightning power, but it is no match against Kai's fiery temper.

BOO!

The gravestones hide a scary secret: there are skeleton soldiers waiting inside!

ROCK HARD

Cole proves his strength when he destroys lots of skeleton soldiers in a surprise attack!

CHARGE!

Kruncha charges into battle, but he doesn't get very far: Cole jumps out of the shadows and clobbers him!

MOST EVIL

Lord Garmadon lets his skeletons do most of the fighting. Then the sneaky villain escapes!

DRAGONS

Four elemental dragons guard the Weapons of Spinjitzu. Earth, Lightning, Fire, and Ice! As the Ninja continue to master their amazing powers, they realize they can control the dragons.

DRAGON ZANE
Zane flies the frosty Ice Dragon to find the lost Shurikens of Ice.

DRAGON KAI
Kai finds his dragon in the Fire Temple. He loves the dragon's heat and energy.

ICE DRAGON
This beautiful but terrifying dragon can freeze attackers with its icy breath. Brrr!

FIRE DRAGON
The Fire Dragon guards the Dragon Sword of Fire. He spits flames at those who try to steal it.

EARTH DRAGON
The mighty Earth Dragon guards the Scythe of Quakes in the Caves of Despair.

DRAGON COLE
Cole used to be afraid of dragons, but now he can control the Earth Dragon!

DRAGON JAY

Jay wears his blue dragon robes when he flies through the air on his speedy Lightning Dragon.

LIGHTNING DRAGON

The Lightning Dragon shoots powerful bolts of electricity to protect the precious Nunchuks of Lightning.

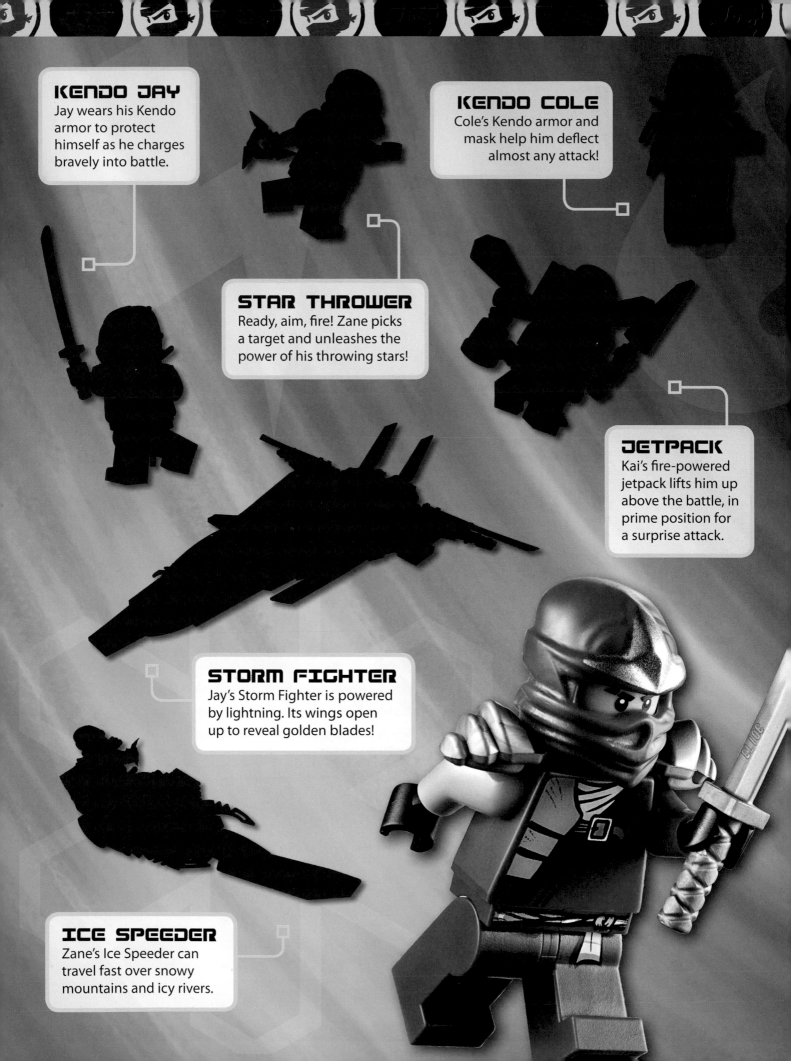

KENDO JAY
Jay wears his Kendo armor to protect himself as he charges bravely into battle.

KENDO COLE
Cole's Kendo armor and mask help him deflect almost any attack!

STAR THROWER
Ready, aim, fire! Zane picks a target and unleashes the power of his throwing stars!

JETPACK
Kai's fire-powered jetpack lifts him up above the battle, in prime position for a surprise attack.

STORM FIGHTER
Jay's Storm Fighter is powered by lightning. Its wings open up to reveal golden blades!

ICE SPEEDER
Zane's Ice Speeder can travel fast over snowy mountains and icy rivers.

NINJA POWER

The Ninja have mastered the incredibly hard sword-fighting skill of Kendo, making them even more powerful. Using their new skills, elemental powers, mystical weapons, and super-charged vehicles, they are unstoppable! Against this Ninja team, no-one stands a chance.

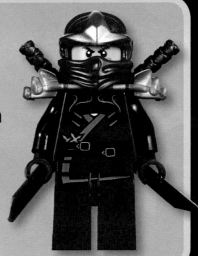

FANG-SUEI FALLS
Fang-Suei gets knocked off his scaly feet by one of Cole's rock missiles.

TREAD ASSAULT
Cole's solid Tread Assault scares the Snakes—it fires huge rock missiles!

NO MATCH
Lord Garmadon has become even more powerful, but he is no match for the Ninja and their weapons!

DESTINY'S BOUNTY
Sensei Wu pilots a flying ship with dragon sails. It is loaded with hidden Ninja weapons!

BLADE CYCLE
Kai rides his red Blade Cycle at super speed! Its sides open out to crush anything in Kai's path.

DANGEROUS SNAKES

The Snakes are cunning, clever, and filled with venom! They want to place everyone in Ninjago under their evil spells. So if you come across a Snake Shrine or a slithering vehicle... run!

SNAPPY

Snappa does more than just bite! He has a curved sword, and he's not afraid to use it!

RATTLECOPTER

Fang-Suei's Rattlecopter has red glowing energy eyes and fires snake missiles.

SNAKE WARS

Fangtom tries to protect his Snake Staff, but Jay won't be easy to defeat!

FANGPYRE TRUCK

Steer clear of Fangdam's monstrous truck! It has a strong, snapping tail and sharp fangs.

VENOMARI

A Snake Staff is housed in the Venomari Shrine, but it is surrounded by traps!

SNEAKY SNAKE

Slithraa plans to distract the Ninja with his blade and then hypnotize them!

BRAINY ZANE

Zane is too strong-minded to be hypnotized. He defeats the evil Snake and finds the Staff!

SNAKE ATTACK

Samurai X is caught off guard by Rattla! Luckily the other Ninja come to the rescue.

RATTLING

Rattla uses all his Snake cunning to attack Samurai X. He rattles his Hypnobrai tail to confuse the Ninja.

LASHING OUT

Lasha isn't scared of the Ninja! He uses a golden ax to defeat his foes.

SHRINE OF SNAKES

Deep in the jungle, the ancient Shrine of Snakes houses one of the precious Snake Staffs.

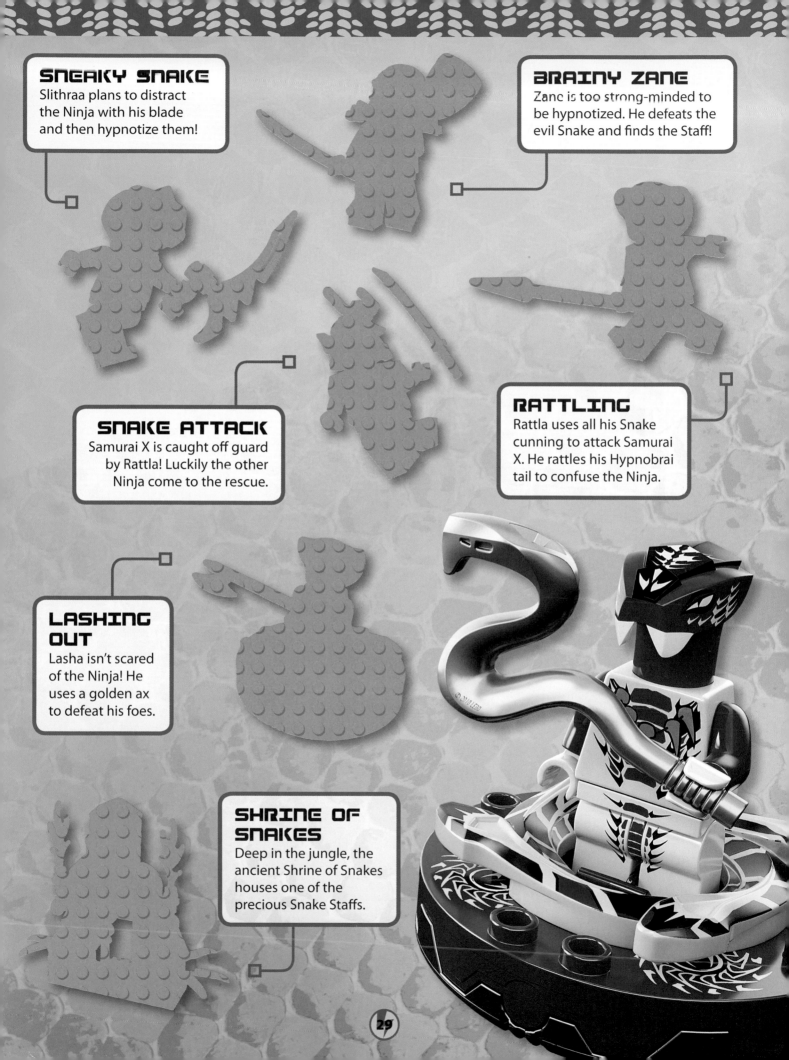

UNDER ATTACK!

Ninjago has been invaded by the Snakes. Can the Ninja defeat the venomous villains? Will they get hold of the golden Snake Staffs? Using all their powers and skills, the Ninja fight back—with fury!

FROSTY
Zane gives the Snakes a frosty reception. His silver katana sword does the rest!

HEATED
Kai leaps straight into battle. He blazes and burns, until all his foes are extinguished.

YOUNG VILLAIN
Lloyd didn't fully realize the danger when he unleashed the Snakes. Now the young villain is in over his head!

EYE CONTACT
Skales uses a silver pike to pin his enemies to the ground. Just don't look into his eyes!

WIDE EYED
When Rattla sees the Ninja, his red eyes go wide! This is one angry Snake!

CALM
Sensei Wu stays calm during battle. He uses his mind to outwit his foes.

NINJA LEADER
Cole leads his team to victory using the Scythe of Quakes. His enemies quake with fear!

THE RETURN
Lord Garmadon returns, offering to help defeat the out-of-control Snakes. Can he be trusted?

JOKESTER
Jay uses his sense of humor to distract his foes. Not so funny now!

COME AND GET IT!
Fangtom taunts the Ninja with his Snake Staff. Big mistake!

PROTECTING NINJAGO

Although the Ninja defeat their enemies, Ninjago is never truly safe. But these brave heroes are well-trained and armed with the Weapons of Spinjitzu—when danger returns, they will be ready!

LIGHTNING!
Jay and the Nunchuks of Lightning guard Ninjago with electric intensity.

EARTH!
Cole always stands strong. The Scythe of Quakes makes him an unstoppable force of nature.

FIRE!
Kai wields the Dragon Sword of Fire with a burning passion to protect Ninjago.

X REVEALED
Samurai X has been revealed—it is Nya! Now a powerful Ninja, Nya is part of the team.

ICE!
Zane uses the chilling powers of the Shurikens of Ice to knock his enemies out cold.

PROUD SENSEI
Sensei Wu is proud of his Ninja students. He fights alongside them to keep Ninjago safe!

Snappy

Fire Spin

Slow Spin

Tread Assault

Shrine of
Snakes

Skull Motorbike

Kruncha

Jay

Blade Cycle

Sneaky
Snake

Family
Team

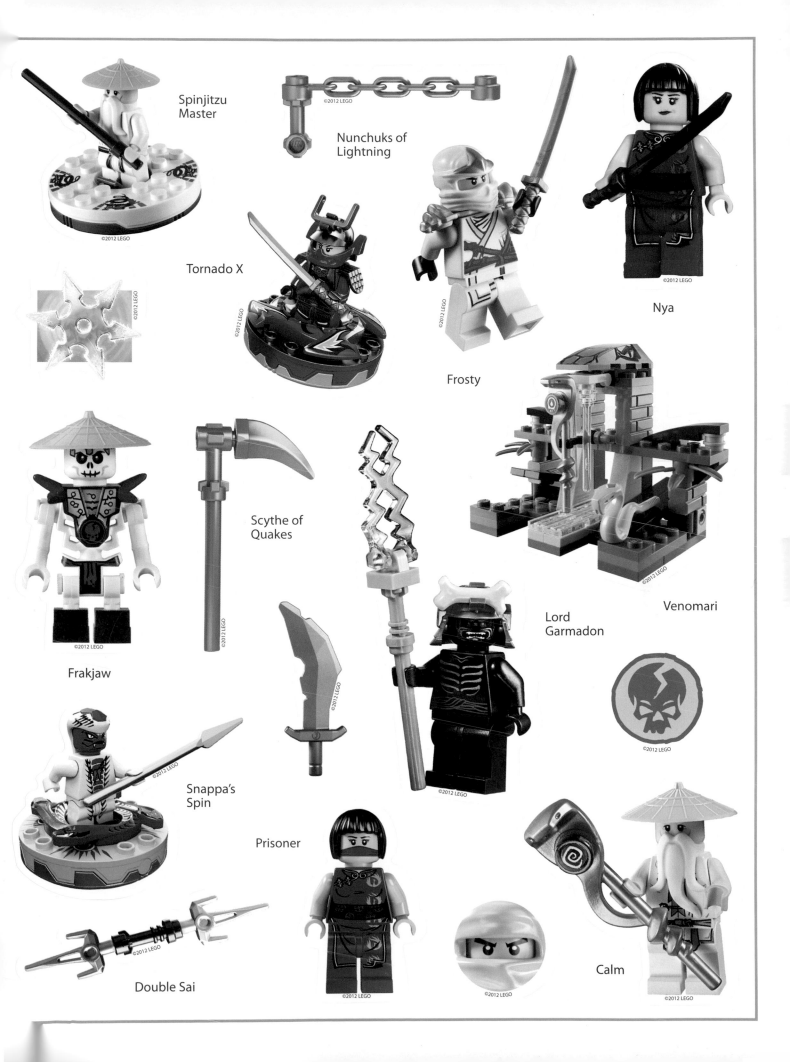

Spinjitzu
Master

Nunchuks of
Lightning

Tornado X

Nya

Frosty

Scythe of
Quakes

Venomari

Lord
Garmadon

Frakjaw

Snappa's
Spin

Prisoner

Double Sai

Calm

Rattla

No Match

Leadership

Lashing
Out

Lightning
Dragon

Dragon Jay

X Revealed

Earth!

Lightning
Spin

Rattlecopter

Snake Wars

Fangpyre
Truck

Dragon Blade

Rattling

Courage

Map of Ninjago

Ninja of
Earth

Dragon
Kai

Shurikens
of Ice

Coordination

Lightning!

Skull Truck

Snappa

©2012 LEGO

Fangtom

Nuckal

Twin
Blades

Jewels

Tornado
of Evil

Chopov

Bullseye!

Heated

Eye
Contact

Brainy Zane

Crushed

Wide Eyed

Ninja Leader

Agility

Sensei Wu

Spinning
Ice

Samukai

Krazi

Cole

Spinjitzu

Young Villain

The Return

Fire Temple

Skeleton of Fire

Nuckal's ATV

Master

Samurai X

Skeleton of Lightning

Beware!

Bladestaff

Behind You!

Practice

Destiny's
Bounty

Cole's Spin

Snake
Attack

Roasting

Meditate

Sword
Skill

Escape

Skeleton of Earth

Come and
Get It!

Ninja
of Fire

New
Weapons

Bone
Claws

Golden Snake

Determination

Mountain
Shrine

Fang-Suei

Snake Staff

Storm Fighter

Ninja of Ice

Fire
Dragon

©2012 LEGO

Team Leader

Boo!

Weapons Master

Kendo Cole

Fighting Mad

Wyplash

Sword of Fire

Kai

Guardian

Bone Spider

Space

Bone
Hammer

Ice
Dragon

Dragon
Sword

Zane

Skullcopter

Stealth

Most Evil

Earth
Dragon

Proud
Sensei

Ice!

Fire!

Snake Pole

Thunderbolt

Wisdom

Charge!

No Fear

Dragon Zane

Fangdam

Dragon Cole

Jokester

Lloyd Garmadon

Chainsaw

Power

Lasha

Captured!

Star Thrower

Skales

Turbo
Shredder

Jetpack

Skeleton
of Ice

Secret Shrine

Greedy Skeleton

Treasure

Ninja of Lightning

Ice Speeder

Bonezai

Chained Fang

Slithraa

Rock Hard

Kendo Jay

Fang-Suei Falls

Defeated

Teamwork

EXTRA STICKERS

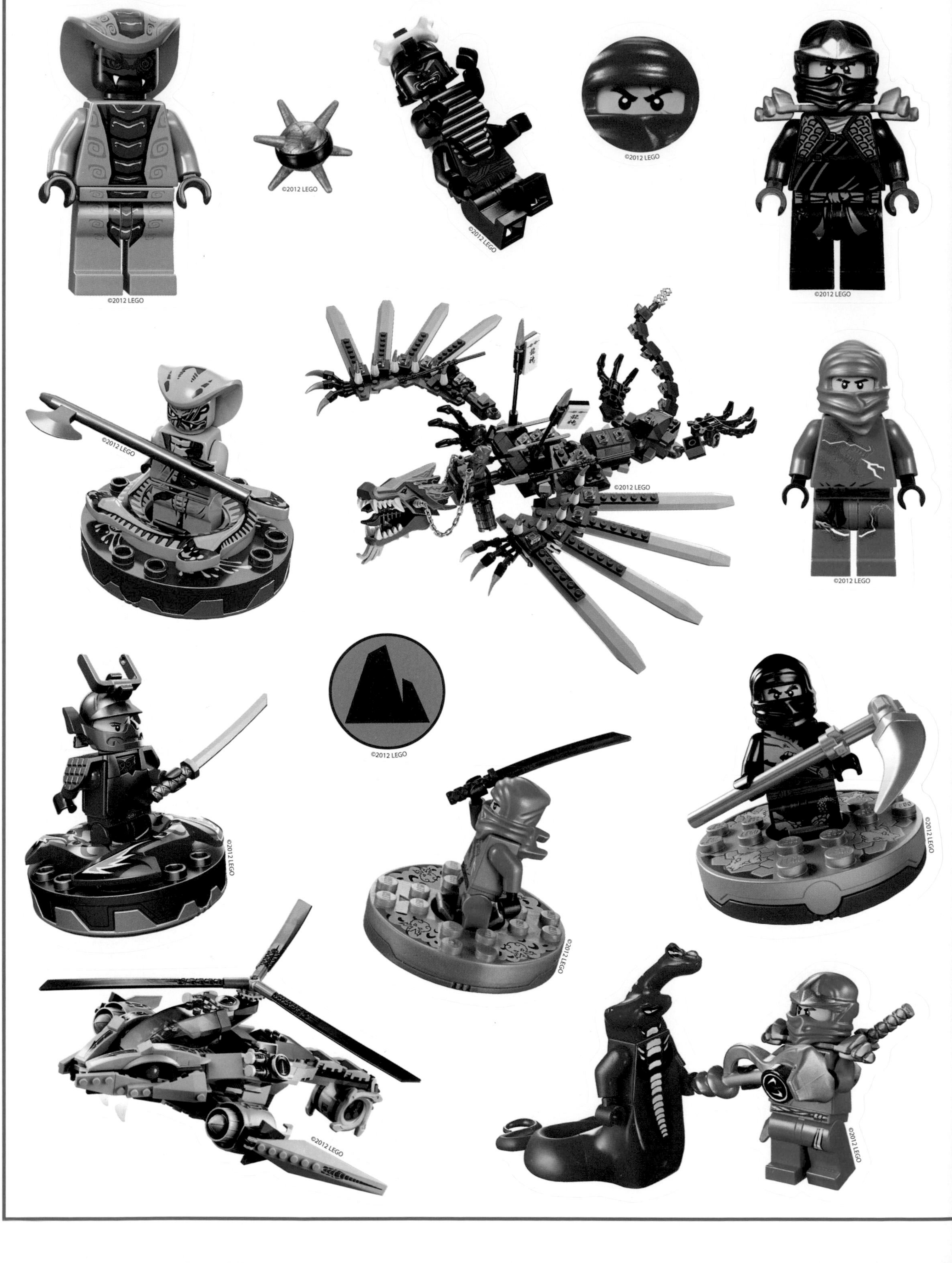

EXTRA STICKERS

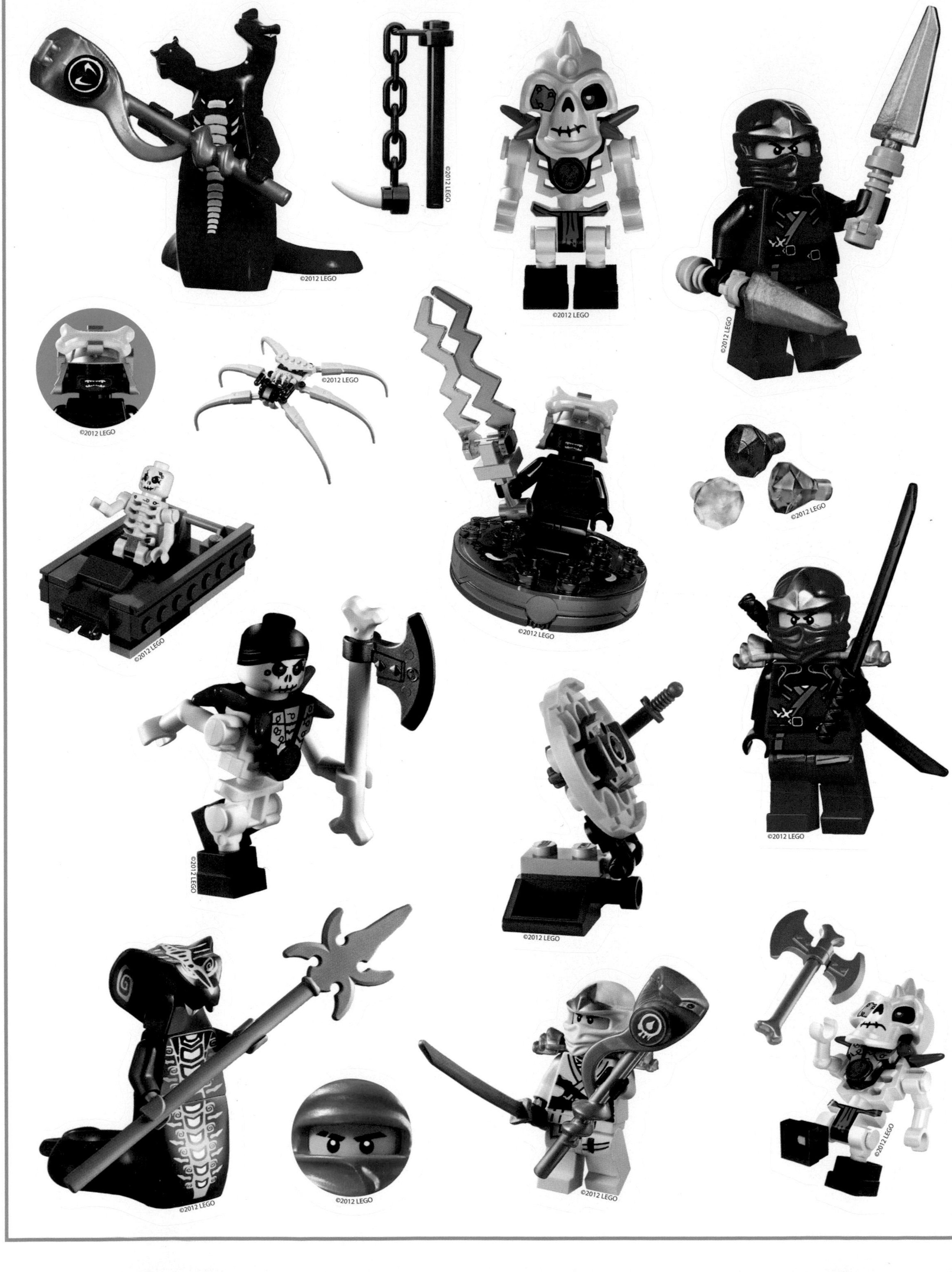

EXTRA STICKERS

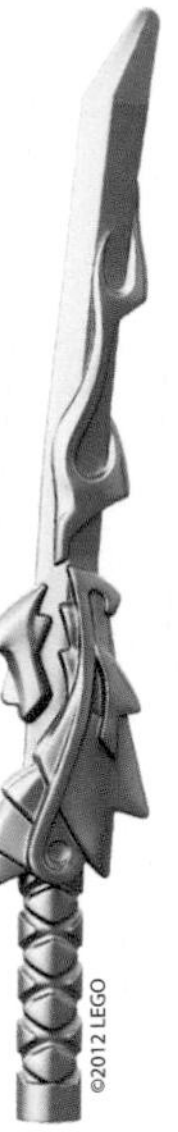

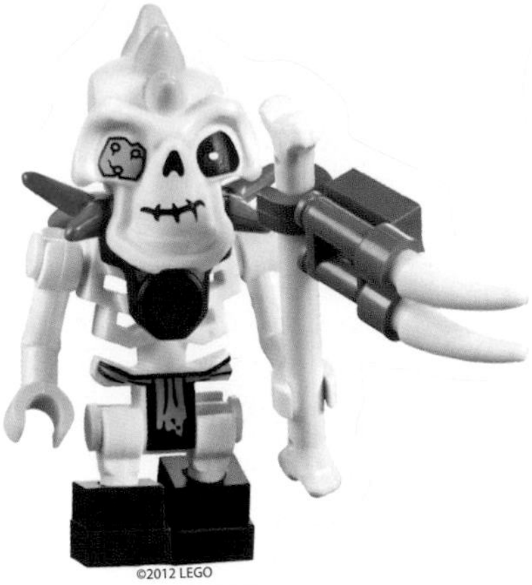

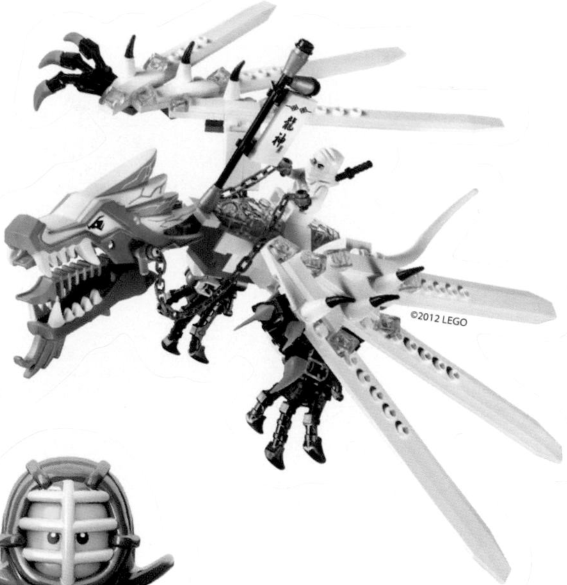

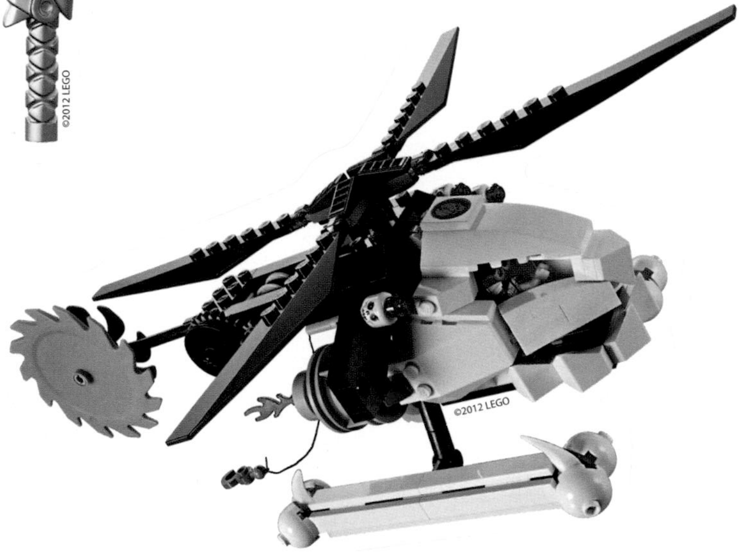

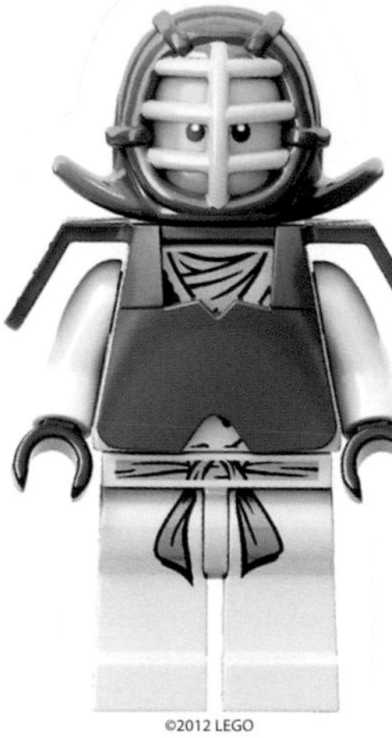

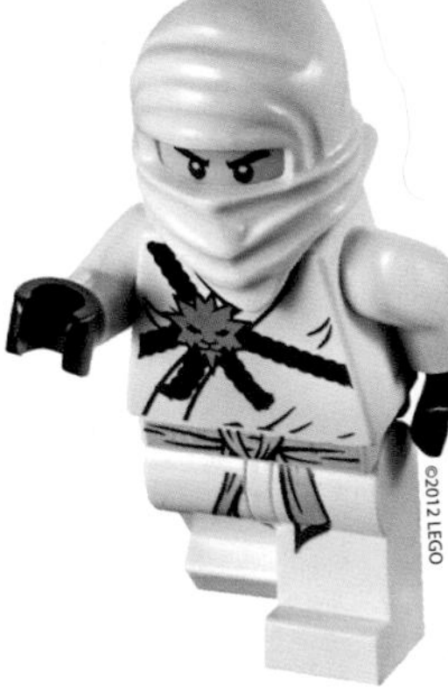

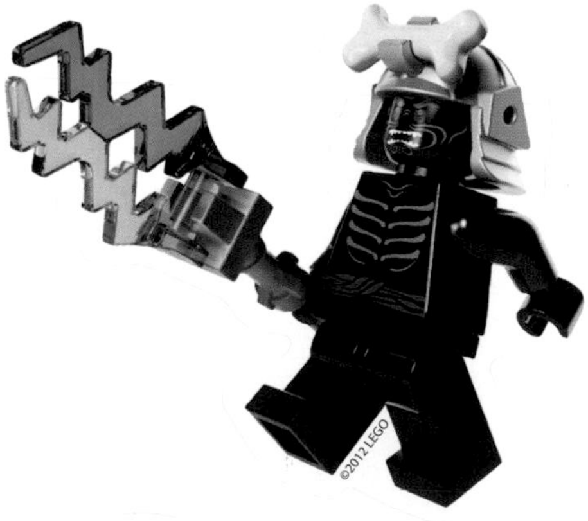

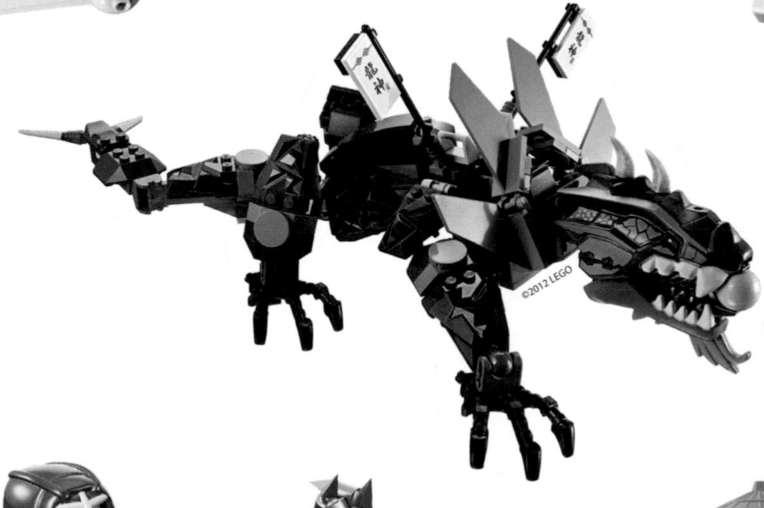

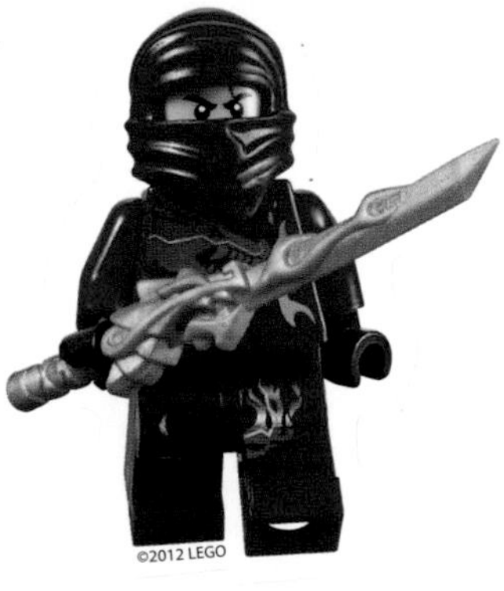

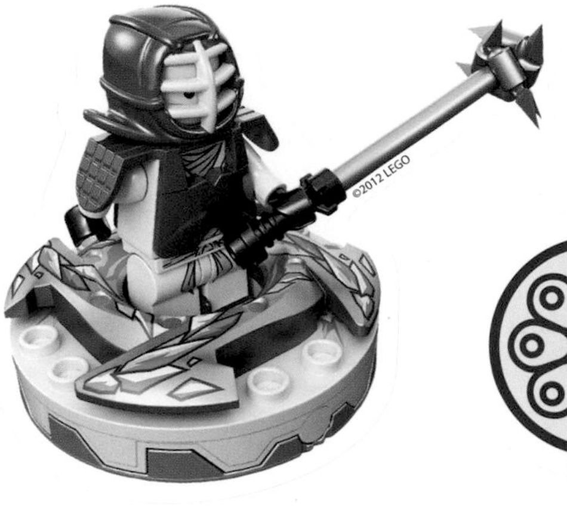

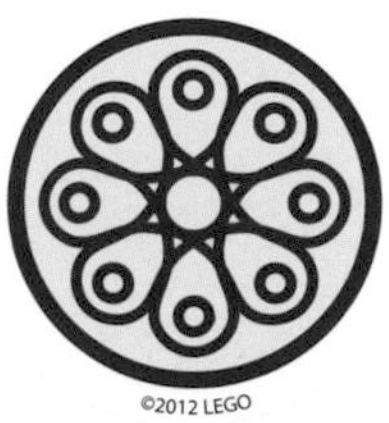

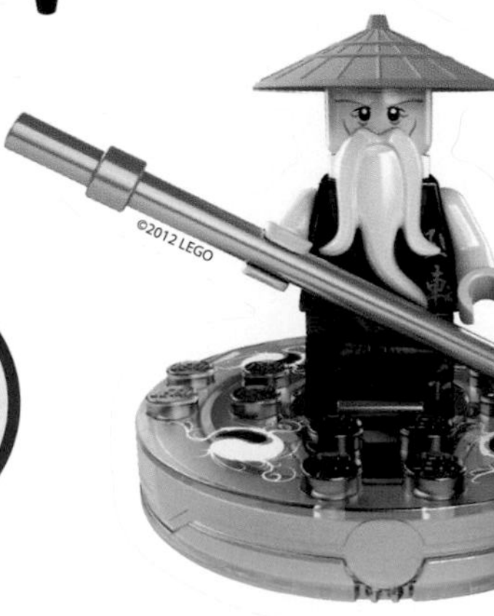

EXTRA STICKERS